This book belongs to:

....

Given by:

....

Date:

....

A Note to Parents

Today your child is taking his or her *First Steps* in the Christian life. This journey is not taken alone. The Bible tells us, "We are surrounded by so great a cloud of witnesses" (Hebrews 12:1), which includes our family, our parish, the angels and saints.

One of the greatest gifts a parent can give a child is a vibrant parish life. In the parish children learn the Faith, devotion to the saints, and reverence for the Divine. It is in the parish where Christian life and friendships are nourished.

Today when busy schedules pull families away from parish life, let us remember the great peace that is found in a community of faith.

As you fill out this baby journal in the weeks and months ahead, let it encourage you to teach your child to walk alongside the saints, both those in your parish and those in heaven.

And let it remind you, and one day your child, of the great gift of Baptism. As Pope Francis says, "We must reawaken the memory of our Baptism. We are called to live out our Baptism every day as the present reality of our lives."

Dedication   **This book is dedicated to all parish priests.**

The author would like to give special thanks to his son, Aiden Gallagher, who came up with the perfect title for this book—further evidence that his insight far surpasses his age.

Text by Conor Gallagher; design and illustration by Chris Pelicano.

Published in the United States by
Saint Benedict Press, LLC
PO Box 410487
Charlotte, NC 28241
www.saintbenedictpress.com
1-800-437-5876

Printed and bound in the U.S.A.
10 9 8 7 6 5 4 3 2

First Steps

In Your Journey of Faith and Parish Life

A Baby Journal from Baptism to First Reconciliation

Saint Benedict Press

Place photo here (sonogram, pregnant mom, family portrait, etc.).

"Before I formed you in the womb, I knew you."

Jeremiah 1:5

PART ONE

Before You Were Formed, You Were Loved

Before God created you,
He knew you as the
fruit of love between
your mother and father.

"Let marriage be held in honor among all."
Hebrews 13:4

Your Parents

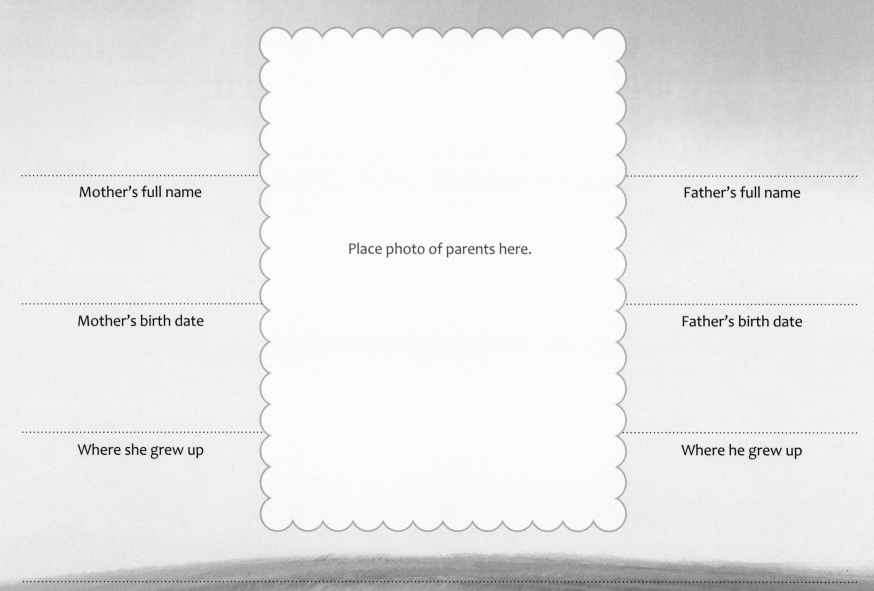

Mother's full name

Father's full name

Place photo of parents here.

Mother's birth date

Father's birth date

Where she grew up

Where he grew up

Comments

Rejoice! A Gift from the Lord

First reactions to the news: ....

....

....

Special feelings about your presence: ....

....

....

What your mother liked to eat when she was pregnant with you: ....

....

....

How your mother felt when she went into labor: ....

....

....

**"God is a Father. Allow Him to act as He pleases.
He knows well what His very small baby needs."**
St. Thérèse of Lisieux

We Call You by Name!

Girl names considered: ....

....

....

Boy names considered: ....

....

....

Your full name: ....

Special significance of your name: ....

....

....

....

....

"I have called you by name, you are mine."

Isaiah 43:1

Getting Ready for You

Place photo here (pregnant mom, baby's room, baby shower, etc.).

Comments

Happy Birthday!

Your birth date is ....

You weighed .... pounds .... ounces.

You were .... inches long.

.... is the person who delivered you.

You were born at .... a.m. p.m. (circle one) in the city of

.... in the state of ....

"This is the day which the Lord has made; let us rejoice and be glad in it."
Psalm 118:24

PART TWO

Made In His Image And Likeness

God made you because He loves.
There is no greater gift than life itself.
You, my child, are a living sign
of God's love and glory.

"Then God said, 'Let us make man in our image, after our likeness.'"
Genesis 1:26

Picturing You!

Place newborn photo here.

"For this child I prayed, and the Lord has granted me my petition."

1 Samuel 1:27

Recalling the Big Day!

What the weather was like: ....

People who were present: ....

....

Length of labor: ....

Feelings when you arrived: ....

....

Family reactions: ....

....

....

Messages sent/messages received: ....

....

"Whoever receives one such child in My name receives Me."
Mark 9:37

Handprints

Place handprints or a photo of your baby's hands below.

"I spread out my hands to You."

Psalm 88:9

Footprints

Place footprints or a photo of your baby's feet below.

"Make straight paths for your feet."
Hebrews 12:13

Place a favorite family photo here.

"The family that prays together, stays together."

PART THREE

A Great Cloud Of Witnesses

You are surrounded
by friends and family
who will both love you and
be a witness of Christ's
love for you.

"We are surrounded by so great a cloud of witnesses."
Hebrews 12:1

"What I love about your mother"

A note from Dad

Why I fell in love with her: ....

....

Her special traits and virtues: ....

....

My favorite story about Mom: ....

....

....

....

....

Blessed Virgin Mary, Mother of God,
pray for us!

"Strength and dignity are her clothing, and she laughs at the time to come."
Proverbs 31:25

"What I love about your father"

A note from Mom

Why I fell in love with him: ....

....

His special traits and virtues: ....

....

My favorite story about Dad: ....

....

....

....

....

St. Joseph, Foster Father of Jesus,
pray for us!

"Hear ... a father's instruction, and be attentive, that you may gain insight."

Proverbs 4:1

Your mother's mother: ....

The nickname you called her: ....

Your mother's father: ....

The nickname you called him: ....

Place photo of baby's
maternal grandparents here.

Your Grandparents

Your father's mother: ....

The nickname you called her: ....

Your father's father: ....

The nickname you called him: ....

Place photo of baby's
paternal grandparents here.

"Old age is a crown of dignity."
Proverbs 16:31 Douay

Great-grandparents

Great-grandparents

....

....

Grandparents

Grandparents

....

Aunts and uncles   **Parents**   Aunts and uncles

....   _____   ....

....   **You**   ....

....   _____

Brothers   Sisters

....

....

....

....

Other family members

....

....

....

Our Family Tree

St. John the Baptist

Patron Saint of Baptism

St. John the Baptist, the patron saint of Baptism, was born to an elderly couple who had never before been able to conceive a child. He was filled with the Holy Spirit even before he was born! An angel promised that he would bring joy to many people, because his miraculous birth was part of God's plan: John was a messenger to prepare the way for the coming of Jesus, the Savior.

Years later, when Jesus began His ministry, He asked John to baptize Him. John obeyed. Then God the Father spoke from heaven, telling the world that Jesus was His beloved Son, and the Holy Spirit came down upon Him. John announced that this innocent "Lamb of God" would take away the sins of the world so they could become holy. He urged others to follow Jesus.

John was later imprisoned and put to death by a wicked king, Herod, because he had publicly challenged Herod to change his ways. John's death, like his entire life, was a powerful witness to God's desire to make us holy. By John's example, he still urges us to follow Jesus.

Prayer to St. John the Baptist

St. John the Baptist, your miraculous birth was a sign of God's faithfulness to your parents and a fulfillment of His promise. Pray for us as we seek to be parents who, in gratitude for this child, are faithful to fulfill the promises we make in this Sacrament of Baptism. You prepared the way for Our Lord Jesus by the witness of your life and your words, and you baptized Him in obedience to His will. Pray for us, that we will prepare the way for this child to know Jesus, to follow Him, and to do His will, not just by the cleansing waters of this Baptism, but through a lifelong witness of our lives, our words, and our loving care as a family. Amen.

PART FOUR

Celebrating Your Baptism

You have taken the first steps
in your journey of faith.
We will always remember this day
as your spiritual birthday,
for you were truly born anew.

"For by one Spirit we were all baptized into one body."
1 Corinthians 12:13

The Day of Your Baptism

Baptism date: ....

Parish: ....

Priest or deacon: ....

People present: ....

....

....

Special memories: ....

....

....

"Baptism is the sacrament of faith. But faith needs the community of believers."
Catechism of the Catholic Church, 1253

Place baptism photo here.

"One Lord, one faith, one baptism."
Ephesians 4:5

Your Godmother

Your godmother's name: ....

How we met her: ....

....

Why we asked her to be your godmother: ....

....

....

....

....

....

Place photo of baby's
godmother here.

Your Godfather

Your godfather's name: ....

How we met him: ....

....

Why we asked him to be your godfather: ....

....

....

....

....

....

....

Place photo of baby's
godfather here.

What the Saints Say About Baptism

Repent and be baptized, every one of you, in the name of Jesus Christ for the forgiveness of your sins; and you will receive the gift of the Holy Spirit. For the promise is to you and your children and to all who are far away, everyone whom the Lord our God calls to Himself.

St. Peter the Apostle

In Christ Jesus you are all children of God through faith. Each of you who were baptized into Christ have put on Christ.

St. Paul the Apostle

Dear parents and godparents, let us entrust to the Virgin Mary's motherly intercession these little ones who are being baptized. Let us ask her to make them, dressed in their white garments, a sign of their new dignity as children of God, true Christians and courageous witnesses to the Gospel throughout their lives.

Pope St. John Paul II

The diver brings up the pearl out of the sea. Be baptized and bring up from the water the purity that is hidden there, the pearl that is set like a jewel in the crown of God.

St. Ephraem the Syrian

After baptism, truth rules the soul.

St. Diadochos of Photiki

Baptism is the vehicle that carries us to God, our dying with Christ, the perfecting of our mind, the bulwark of faith, the key of the kingdom of heaven, the transformation of our life, the liberation from our slavery, the loosing of our chains, the renovation of our whole nature. Why should I go into further detail? The illumination of Baptism is the greatest and most magnificent of the gifts of God.

St. Gregory Nazianzen

"The soul is reborn in the sacred waters of baptism and thus becomes God's child."

St. Maximilian Kolbe

Baptism is a gift bestowed by means of something we can perceive with our senses, that is, water. But the reality of what takes place in Baptism is perceived by the mind instead; I mean the spiritual birth, the renewal, that it brings.

St. John Chrysostom

The sacrament of Baptism is most certainly the sacrament of rebirth.

St. Augustine

The Holy Spirit blesses the body that is baptized and the water that baptizes. So don't consider the water used in Baptism as something common and of little value. For the divine power that operates through the water is mighty, and the things that are accomplished through it are wonderful.

St. Gregory of Nyssa

Being reborn from above by water and the Spirit, in Christ we are all made alive.

St. Athanasius

I baptize you with water ... but He will baptize you with the Holy Spirit and fire.

St. John the Baptist

Baptism is the sacrament of faith.

St. Thomas Aquinas

It is beneficial to celebrate the anniversary of your Baptism by lighting your baptismal candle and, with your family, renewing your promises to renounce sin and live as a faithful follower of Jesus Christ and His Church.

"Baptism is . . . a chariot to heaven!"
St. Basil the Great

Place your favorite
"baby's first time" photo here.

"Let the children come to me."
Matthew 19:14

PART FIVE

First-Time Memories At Home

Our first memories of you
have been a blessing.
We thank God for each and
every moment with you.

"But Mary kept all these things, pondering them in her heart."

Luke 2:19

✝ First Smile ✝

Date: ....

How it made me feel: ....

....

"The eye that smiles, how it cheers the heart!"
Proverbs 15: 30 Knox

✝ Sitting Up ✝

Date: ....

What it was like seeing you sit up: ....

....

You are ready to sit at the feet of Jesus!

✝ Crawling ✝

Date: ....

Where you started to go: ....

....

"Let us kneel before the LORD, our Maker!"
Psalm 95:6

✝ First Meal of Solid Food ✝

Date: ....

What you ate: ....

....

"I am the Lord your God … Open your mouth wide, and I will fill it."
Psalm 81:10

✝ First Words ✝

Hearing you say your very first words was exciting and wonderful. Here are some of those words.

Word: .... Date: ....

Comments: ....

Word: .... Date: ....

Comments: ....

Word: .... Date: ....

Comments: ....

Word: .... Date: ....

Comments: ....

Word: .... Date: ....

Comments: ....

"Let the words of my mouth ... be acceptable."
Psalm 19:14

✝ First Steps ✝

Date you took your first steps: ....

Where you were: ....

Who you walked to: ....

What you looked like as you tried to walk: ....

....

....

....

....

....

"Keep steady my steps according to Your promise."

Psalm 119:133

St. Anthony of Padua

The Saint Who Held Baby Jesus

St. Anthony of Padua is the patron saint of the poor and of those who need help finding something that has been lost. He is one of the most popular of Catholic saints—perhaps because so many people need his help!

Born in Lisbon, Portugal, in 1195, Anthony was the son of a knight in the royal court. But he gave up the honors and comforts of courtly life to enter religious life instead, and eventually became a Franciscan priest in Italy. Anthony soon earned fame as a brilliant preacher; his sermons convinced thousands of people to give their lives to God. He was also known for his devoted service to the poor.

One night as Anthony was praying, his room was filled with light, and Jesus appeared to him as a little Child. Someone passing by saw the saint holding the holy Babe in his arms and talking to Him. So pictures of Anthony usually show him this way, and he has become a favorite saint among children.

Anthony performed so many miracles that people called him the "Wonder Worker." He died in 1231 and was later declared a Doctor (Teacher) of the Church.

Prayer to St. Anthony

St. Anthony, you loved the Child Jesus and once held Him in your arms; show your love for this child by holding him/her in your prayers. You are the helper of those who have lost something; be ready to help this child whenever he/she calls on you to find what has been lost. You cared deeply for all those in need; teach this child to care for those in need. And just as you called on people everywhere to give their lives to God, let your words and your example lead this child to God. St. Anthony, thank you for being the friend of children everywhere! Amen.

St. Anthony, help us not lose these memories!

Dear St. Anthony,

During these first years of our child's life we've seen God's goodness in so many ways. We've seen our child learn to walk, learn to talk, and become an irreplaceable part of our family. Help us never lose these memories.

In these first few years, we've come to see why the kingdom of God belongs to little children. Help our own child never lose hold of the innocence needed to obtain eternal life. Amen.

St. Anthony, patron saint of lost articles, pray for our child!

Our Parish

Our parish name: ....

Why we love our parish: ....

....

Our pastor's name: ....

Special friends in our parish community: ....

....

....

....

....

"There are many parts, yet one body."

1 Corinthians 12:20

PART SIX

First Steps In Your Life Of Faith

We will walk together
through your journey of faith.
We have chosen our parish as the path.
This community of believers
will show us the way.

"You cannot pray at home as at church."
Catechism of the Catholic Church, 2179

Your First Christmas!

Memories of your first Christmas Mass: ....

....

....

....

Your first Christmas presents: ....

....

Family and friends with whom we shared Christmas: ....

....

....

....

....

"Glory to the newborn King!"

Joy to the World!

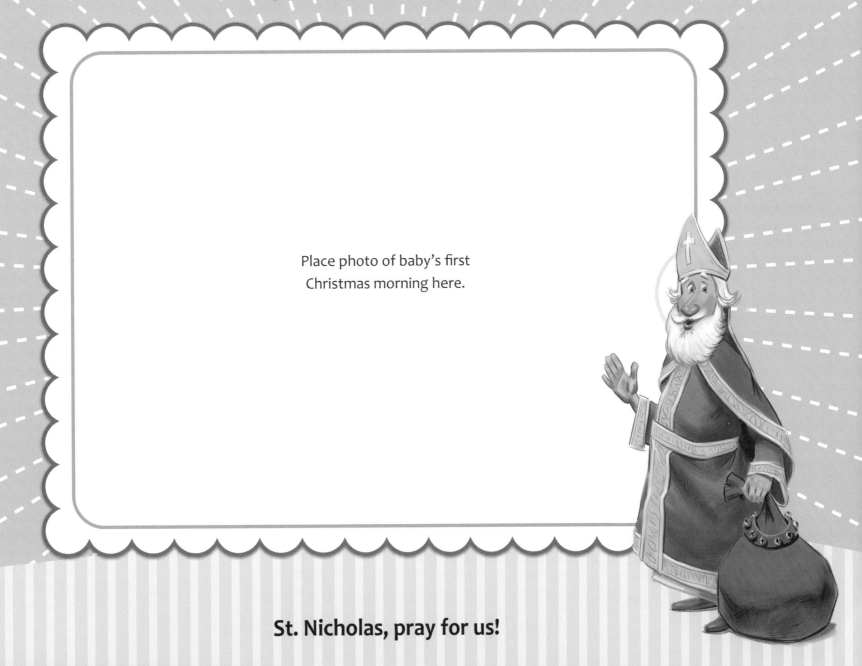

Place photo of baby's first
Christmas morning here.

St. Nicholas, pray for us!

Your First Easter!

Memories of your first Easter Mass: ....

....

....

....

Your first Easter basket or presents: ....

....

Family and friends with whom we shared Easter: ....

....

....

....

....

"I am the resurrection and the life."

John 11:25

Hallelujah!

Place photo of baby's first
Easter morning here.

Christ is risen! He is truly risen!

Special Memories of Parish Life

The Mass we usually attended: ....

The place where we usually sat at Mass: ....

How you reacted to being at Mass: ....

....

Fellow parishioners about your age: ....

....

Some special parish events you attended during your first year: ....

....

....

....

....

"Let us consider how to stir up one another to love and good works, not neglecting to meet together."
Hebrews 10:24-25

Our Parish and Community

How our parish helps the poor: ....

....

How our parish helps young people: ....

....

Special ministries (e.g., Knights of Columbus, St. Vincent de Paul Society): ....

....

....

Ways our family can get more involved: ....

....

....

....

"As each one has received a gift, employ it for one another as good stewards of God's varied grace."

1 Peter 4:10

St. Brigid of Ireland
Patron Saint of Infants

St. Brigid, the patron saint of infants, was born in Ireland about the year 453. From a young age, she developed a habit of giving her wealthy household's food to the poor. When her father, who disapproved of her generosity, sought to find her a husband, she consecrated herself to Christ instead and became a nun.

Brigid's personal holiness drew others to her, and when she was fifteen, she established a religious community with seven other young women joining her. Appointed as abbess by the local bishop, she eventually founded a number of monasteries that served the poor and the sick and provided hospitality. The most famous of these, at Kildare, also became famous as a great center of learning and art.

Many miracles were attributed to Brigid's intercession. Several of these involved children, and one legend even claims that she miraculously granted an infant, too young to speak, the power to answer a question she was asked. Perhaps that is why she is known as the patron of infants.

Brigid died in 525, having left a lasting imprint throughout Ireland and beyond. Along with St. Patrick, she is recognized as a patron saint of that country.

St. Brigid's Blessing

May Brigid bless the house in which you dwell;

Bless every fireside, every wall and door;

Bless every heart that beats beneath its roof;

Bless every hand that toils to bring it joy;

Bless every foot that walks its portals through;

May Brigid bless the house that shelters you.

—*Traditional Irish blessing*

PART SEVEN

Growing In Age And Grace

As we watch you
grow in age and grace,
we will, as a family,
grow in holiness.

"Grow in the grace and knowledge of our Lord and Savior Jesus Christ."
2 Peter 3:18

1st-Year Memories!

Words and phrases you used the most: ....

....

Some of the great things you learned to do: ....

....

Family members you spent a lot of time with: ....

....

Your favorites (foods/activities/books/toys): ....

....

Funniest story about you from your first year: ....

....

....

....

You certainly didn't feel well at times.

Spiritual Growth!

A Child's Prayer

Come gracious Spirit, heavenly Dove,

With light and comfort from above.

Be Thou our Guardian, Thou our Guide,

Stay close by every child's side. Amen!

Mom's favorite prayer for you: ....

....

....

Dad's favorite prayer for you: ....

....

....

St. Polycarp, pray for us!
Patron Saint of Earaches

2nd-Year Memories!

When and where you took your first steps: ....

....

When you pointed to your nose, ears, eyes: ....

....

The sounds and actions you imitated: ....

....

Your favorites (sweets/playmates/songs/foods): ....

....

Your very first sentences: ....

....

....

....

You had some days that weren't too happy.

Spiritual Growth!

When and how you learned to fold your hands in prayer: ....

....

When you learned to say "Amen": ....

....

A little comment on learning to say "Jesus": ....

....

Other important religious words or concepts you are learning (e.g., "Mommy Mary" or "Jesus loves me"):

....

....

....

St. Apollonia, pray for us!
Patron Saint of Teething

3rd-Year Memories!

The most amazing thing you learned this year: ....

....

How you have shown affection: ....

....

How you have shown frustration: ....

....

Your favorites (clothes/objects of endearment/people/places to go): ....

....

One of the sweetest things you did all year: ....

....

....

....

Your happiness was contagious at times.

Spiritual Growth!

How did you learn to sit through Mass? ....

....

How did you learn to make the Sign of the Cross? ....

....

Any funny stories about being in church? ....

....

....

How are you doing with "Please" and "Thank you"? ....

....

Bible stories we have begun to tell you: ....

....

St. Francis of Assisi, pray for us!
Patron Saint of Animals

4th-Year Memories!

The interesting pictures you drew this year: ....

....

How high can you count? ....

....

A poem we really liked: ....

....

Your favorites (colors/games/new activities/drinks): ....

....

You and your make-believe: ....

....

....

....

When you hurt, we prayed for you.

Spiritual Growth!

When and how you learned the "Hail Mary": ....

....

How you are doing at mealtime prayer: ....

....

Are you learning to share your toys? ....

....

Are you misbehaving at bedtime? ....

....

Other spiritual progress you made this year: ....

....

St. Colette, pray for us!
Patron Saint of Sick Children

5th-Year Memories!

The names of some of your best friends: ....

....

Have you learned your alphabet? ....

....

Your favorite books: ....

....

Your favorite activities: ....

....

The most endearing story of your fifth year: ....

....

....

....

St. John Bosco, pray for us!
Patron Saint of Boys

✝ Spiritual Growth! ✝

How your "Our Father" is coming along: ....

....

Are you obeying Mom and Dad? ....

....

Other ways you are showing good manners: ....

....

....

How you are behaving at bedtime: ....

....

....

St. Maria Goretti, pray for us!
Patron Saint of Girls

6th-Year Memories!

Your favorite activity in school: ....

....

Your strongest personality trait: ....

....

The movie that you want to watch over and over: ....

....

Your interesting choice of clothes: ....

....

The funniest moment of the year: ....

....

....

You had lots to celebrate!

Spiritual Growth!

New ways you have learned to help Mom and Dad around the house: ....

....

Have you learned to clean up your mess? ....

....

Are you eating your vegetables? ....

....

New prayers you are learning to say: ....

....

Your favorite Bible stories: ....

....

....

St. Benedict, pray for us!
Patron Saint of School Children

7th-Year Memories!

Your favorite subject in school: ....

....

The things you can do all by yourself: ....

....

Your favorite sport: ....

....

Your favorite relatives: ....

....

The happiest moment of the year: ....

....

....

You taught us as much as we taught you.

Spiritual Growth!

Have you learned to ask forgiveness when you are wrong? ....

....

Have you learned to say your bedtime prayers on your own? ....

....

Chores we have given you and how you are doing with them: ....

....

Things you are "giving up" for Lent: ....

....

The things we have done to prepare for the Sacrament of Reconciliation: ....

....

....

St. (Padre) Pio, pray for us!
Help us make a good confession!

Getting Ready for the Sacrament of Reconciliation

Your parents had you baptized because they love you. It was the greatest gift they could give you: better than toys or money or any other treat. Baptism is a gift that will last forever and ever. It was the beginning of your life as a child of God, and God's children will live in heaven for all eternity!

Baptism is what we call a *sacrament*. This means that the actions of the priest or deacon are signs of what God is doing inside you. In your baptism, as the priest or deacon poured water over your head to wash your body, the Holy Spirit came down from heaven to wash your soul.

Since that time, your family and your parish have helped you learn to know Jesus, to love Him, and to trust Him. At home and at church, they have taught you how to pray, how to worship at Mass, and how to make the right choices. Now, as you are getting older, the time has come for you to take another important step in your life as a child of God. This time, your parents can't do for it for you; you must do it yourself.

You are now old enough to know the difference between right and wrong. You also know that when you do something wrong, you must ask God and others to forgive you and to help you not sin again. God has made a way, through the Church, for you to do just that. It's called the *Sacrament of Reconciliation*, and it's also known as *Confession* or *Penance*.

In this sacrament, the priest listens as you confess your sins to God and ask Him to forgive you. Then the priest speaks to you for God, telling you that your sins are forgiven. Finally, the priest asks you to do some small act (such as a prayer or a good deed) that will help you do the right thing next time.

Your soul needs to be washed clean by Baptism only once. But you can go to Reconciliation as often as you need to ask God for forgiveness. When you do, your soul is clean all over again!

Now you know a little about the Sacrament of Reconciliation. In the days to come, you'll learn much more about how to get ready for this wonderful gift from God that brings you closer to Him.

"Conversion entails both God's forgiveness and reconciliation with the Church."
Catechism of the Catholic Church, 1440

Your First Reconciliation

Date: ....

Parish: ....

Priest: ....

What was it like? ....

....

....

....

....

"Conversion is first of all a work of the grace of God who makes our hearts return to him."

Catechism of the Catholic Church, 1432

Prayer to Your Guardian Angel

Angel of God, my guardian dear, to whom God's love commits me here, ever this day, be at my side, to light and guard, to rule and guide. Amen.

A Short Litany of the Saints

St. John the Baptist, pray for us!

St. Polycarp, pray for us!

St. Apollonia, pray for us!

St. Nicholas, pray for us!

St. Brigid, pray for us!

St. Benedict, pray for us!

St. Francis of Assisi, pray for us!

St. Anthony of Padua, pray for us!

St. Colette, pray for us!

St. John Bosco, pray for us!

St. Thérèse of Lisieux, pray for us!

St. Maria Goretti, pray for us!

St. (Padre) Pio, pray for us!

St. Joseph, pray for us!

Holy Mary, Mother of God, pray for us!

All holy angels and saints, pray for us!